THE UNOFFICIAL

John Travolta

BY
Rachel Simpson

This edition first published by
Parragon Book Service Ltd in 1996

Parragon Book Service Ltd
Unit 13–17 Avonbridge Trading Estate
Atlantic Road, Avonmouth
Bristol BS11 9QD

Produced by Magpie Books,
an imprint of Robinson Publishing

Copyright © Parragon Book Service Ltd 1996

All rights reserved. This book is sold subject to the
condition that it shall not, by way of trade or otherwise,
be lent, resold, hired out or otherwise circulated
without the publisher's prior consent in any form of
binding or cover other than that in which it is published
and without similar condition being imposed on
the subsequent purchaser.

ISBN 0 75251 793 7

A copy of the British Library Cataloguing in Publication
Data is available from the British Library.

Typeset by Whitelaw & Palmer Ltd, Glasgow

'MOMMA, I WANT TO BE A STAR'

John Travolta is the original come-back kid. As a swivel-hipped 24-year-old in the seventies, he put himself, the Bee Gees and the whole art of disco-dancing on the map in *Saturday Night Fever*. He was an overnight sensation, became a multi-millionaire, and went on the following year to capitalise on his success, in *Grease*.

Saturday Night Fever, talking to Karen Lynn Gorney

And then what happened? What indeed? Thrown off course by the deaths of his mother and his lover, Travolta made a handful of flops, and was all but dropped by Hollywood. Indeed, a few years ago, he was ready to jack in acting and take up a career as an airline pilot. That was when a brash young director called Quentin Tarantino found him, and cast him as a hip, happening, hit man in *Pulp Fiction*. It was such a success that Travolta is now the highest paid film star in the world.

John Travolta was born with acting in his blood. His mother Helen, whose pretty blue eyes betrayed her Irish ancestry, had first made her debut on the stage at the age of nine. As her son would be 40 years later, she was hooked on acting from then on.

Helen and her family lived in New Jersey, the American state which is separated from New York by the Hudson River. It was while at school there, as a pretty teenager, that she first set eyes on a boy called Salvatore Travolta, the son of an Italian immigrant. Salvatore was not just a school hero because of his footballing talents. He also possessed striking good looks which, the besotted Helen thought, gave him a distinct resemblance to Cary Grant. They met, started dating, and were soon inseparable.

As it turned out, this was no ordinary teenage romance. Helen and Salvatore stayed in love even when Salvatore – or Sam, as his friends called him – went off to college on a footballing scholarship, and Helen headed to Columbia University to study drama. After they graduated, when Helen was 26, they married. Sam set out on a career as a semi-professional footballer, and Helen devoted her time to drama. She had a performing radio group called 'The Sunshine Sisters', and also found work teaching drama in the New Jersey high schools. She was no mean actress herself: her performances in plays like Thornton Wilder's *Our Town* brought her comparisons with stars like Barbara Stanwyck.

Soon after their wedding, Sam and Helen started a family, and by the time Helen was 42, they had five children – three girls and two boys. So the day Helen discovered she was pregnant again, she was rather shocked. She felt that she was getting a little old to be going through a pregnancy – with all its problems of morning sickness and fatigue – all over again. But when the new arrival, a boy, appeared at 2 pm on 18 February 1954, Helen changed her mind about having another child. As he grew up, inheriting his father's cleft chin, dimples and hair and his mother's big blue eyes, Helen – as many women after her would – decided that John Joseph Travolta was rather cute.

The new baby was brought home to a large house on a tree-lined street in Englewood, New Jersey. This was a pleasant and thriving town of about 25,000 inhabitants, half an hour's drive from New York City. Although the Travoltas weren't rich – Sam had now given up football, and was running a large tyre shop in the town with his brother – they had enough money to get by. The house was a comfortable family home with a garden, where John would play football. His sisters, he discovered, took after their mother in showing more interest in drama than football. When he was growing up, Ellen, Margaret and Ann would dress him up as a girl in their old clothes, and cast him as a character in the little plays they put on. They would even put make-up on him. By the time John was nine, all three of his older sisters were acting professionally.

One of John's earliest memories was of seeing off his oldest sister Ellen at the airport every time she left town for an acting job. For this reason, the little boy became convinced that acting and flying were naturally linked together. Lying awake in bed at night, he too longed to be able to fly off to exciting destinations. New Jersey lay on the flight path for any jet headed westbound from New York, so the young John would listen to the planes flying overhead at a height of 2,000 feet and climbing, and wonder who was on board and where they were going. It stimulated an early interest in planes.

All the children were now showing an interest in performing. John's two brothers Joey and Sam Jr both enjoyed pop and rock music, and music was always playing in the house. John grew up to the sound of Elvis, The Beach Boys, and the Beatles, and soon took an active interest in both acting and dancing.

From as young as two, John would

interrupt Helen's housework to ask, 'Momma, can we sit down and play-act?' She would drop the ironing or dusting, or whatever she was doing for a few minutes, and invent a little scene for the two of them to act out. Within a couple of years, she was taking him with her when she went to coach drama at the Englewood schools. He loved watching his mother's student productions. Back at home, he would mimic and sing along to the records his parents kept, and dance in front of the television whenever old musicals – such as the James Cagney film *Yankee Doodle Dandy* – were shown on TV.

By the age of five, John was asking how he too could end up on stage, in a musical. When he asked for dancing lessons, Helen enrolled him in a tap-dancing class, with one of the best dance teachers she could find: Fred Kelly, brother of *Singin' in the Rain* star, Gene. John was soon demonstrating early promise as a dancer, and became one of Fred's favourite pupils.

By this time, his big sister Ellen had got a part in a touring production of *Gypsy*, starring the legendary Ethel Merman. Although John was only six, Ellen decided to test out his early fascination with the stage, and invited him along to the show's opening in Chicago. John was thrilled. A chance to see a real musical! And even more exciting, the chance to fly in a real plane to Chicago! Ellen told John that if he behaved himself, she would treat him to his first ever (and completely illicit) glass of wine, but he was so enthralled, he needed no bribes to be good.

Going to see *Gypsy* only confirmed John's view that he wanted to join his sisters on the stage. 'Momma,' he would tell Helen eagerly, 'I want to be a star.' Back in New Jersey, he continued the dancing lessons, and at the age of eight showed such promise that he was pushed onto the stage at Englewood's annual fireworks party to dance. 'Ladies and gentleman,' the master of ceremonies announced, 'Englewood Yearly Fireworks presents that dance craze, The Twist, danced by little Johnny Travolta.' John got up on stage and started gyrating, just as he had seen dancers on the TV do.

John was now twelve, and like his brothers and sisters before him, he was doing a few paid chores to bring extra cash into the household. He delivered groceries and repaired furniture, but his main interest was still acting. Helen decided he was old enough to attend an audition and sent John to try out for a part in a community production of a drama called *Who'll Save the Ploughboy?* He was successful and won a small part as a child. He only had to speak a few lines in his first ever role, but his proud mother said, 'He spoke them so meaningfully, he stole the show.' Though she didn't know it at the time, it was a foretaste of things to come.

John Travolta in *Welcome Back Kotter*

BYE BYE, BIRDIE

When the adult John Travolta first found fame as the star of the American teenage sitcom *Welcome Back Kotter*, his old high school put him in their hall of fame. This move surprised him, for as a student at the Dwight Morrow Public High School, less than a mile away from his home, John Travolta didn't exactly cover himself with glory.

It wasn't that he was stupid. It was more that he was uninterested. His heart was so set on singing and dancing that working for top grades at school came a poor second. Instead, he became a bit of a class clown: he liked a laugh; he enjoyed fooling around and making fun of his teachers, largely because he was bored.

More enjoyable than lessons was the atmosphere of the school. This was the swinging sixties: the world was going through huge changes, and so was the music, ranging from the Beatles to Motown. Music was always playing in the corridors between lessons, somebody always had a radio and was dancing along to the newest songs being played on the air. Many of the pupils enjoyed dancing – John's brother Joey was a regular winner of the school dance contests – but John made a point of heading for the black pupils to copy their moves from them. It seemed to him that they had a looser style – and a better sense of humour. At the time, he didn't think he was doing anything more than having fun, but learning how to wiggle his hips the way other white boys couldn't, would later stand him in very good stead.

There was some compensation for the boredom of lessons in the school social life. John discovered girls. He also discovered that he was attracted to far more of them than ever returned the compliment. In 1968, at the age of 14, he fell in love with a beautiful brunette called Denise. She was tall – five foot eight – and like John, a good dancer. She made it obvious that she thought he was very good looking, and after being rejected by many other girls, the young John found that very attractive.

By now John was travelling regularly to see his sisters perform in whatever play or summer repertory show they were in. And at the age of 16, he decided it was about time he started going to some auditions himself: after all, he was spending enough time practising his singing and taking dancing lessons. He thought that now was as good a time as any to put his hard work to good use.

And so in the summer of 1970, he went to an audition at a theatre in New Jersey. They were looking for actors for a new production of a play called *Bye Bye, Birdie*, which had formerly been a smash hit on Broadway. John read his lines and danced and sang for the director as though his life depended on it. It paid off: he landed the second lead in the show, along with a princely salary of $50 a week.

At first his parents were delighted. After all, as this was the summer holidays, performing in the show wouldn't affect his school work. As supportive parents who had always encouraged his creative tendencies, they were delighted to see him do well. What they didn't know was that trouble was brewing.

The first indication of trouble was when he was spotted by an agent. John had an unglamorous role, as a plain lad who loses his girlfriend when an Elvis Presley-like rock and roll star called Conrad Birdie arrives in town. A new York agent called Bob LeMond came to the show one night, initially with the intention of seeing another member of the cast. But after watching Travolta perform, he forgot all about his other 'hopeful'. After the show was over, he went backstage and introduced himself. When John wanted advice about starting a full-time acting career, LeMond said, he should come to him.

Partly because of Bob LeMond's intervention, and partly because John was being paid to do something he really enjoyed for the first time in his life, he couldn't bear the thought of having to quit the stage at the end of the summer and go back to school. So when the show finished, he asked his parents' permission to be allowed to drop out of school.

His mother Helen agreed more readily than his father. Sam was upset by John's request, saying that although he had auditioned and won one part, there were no guarantees that he would be able to make a career for himself in acting. A stormy meeting between father and son ensued, and at one point, John burst into tears. In the end, his father relented. 'All right,' he agreed. 'You go out and do your thing. But if you don't succeed in one year, you must agree that you will come back and finish school.' John accepted the deal.

When *Bye Bye Birdie*, finished, he rang Bob LeMond and went to see him in New York. LeMond was as helpful and encouraging as he had been when he first spotted Travolta. And he kept his newest client busy, sending John to auditions and casting calls. He also sent him to try out for commercials. Even back in 1971, a young actor could earn a few thousand dollars a time for making TV adverts – a small fortune to a penniless youngster just starting out. He won quite a few parts: in between attending his dancing and acting classes, John extolled the virtues of everything from soft drinks to insurance, from sticking plasters to motorbikes. In the summer of 1971, he also won a small role in a stage production of *The Boyfriend*. By now, his father Sam had to accept that John wouldn't be going back to school. 'What can I say?,' Sam told his son proudly, 'You did it.'

Up to this point, John had been living at home in Englewood, sleeping in his room in the attic, practising his dancing downstairs in the big room in the basement. But now the strain of commuting was taking its toll. Every day he had to make the journey into New York for acting classes, or to film a commercial, and he decided that he needed a place of his own – *in* New York. Although he was only 17 his parents agreed, because his first apartment was shared with his older sister, Ann. John stayed with her while he hunted for somewhere of his own to live, and he and a group of buddies soon ended up renting an apartment in the tough New York area of Hell's Kitchen. The heating didn't work very well and the lift was broken. In fact, the only thing it offered in abundance was cockroaches.

Although he wasn't living like a lord, Travolta was doing well in his new career. Casting directors liked this fresh-faced young lad with dark wavy hair. Soon, as well as doing commercials, he was finding work in off-Broadway shows. He also landed a couple of small parts in television soap operas. They didn't make his name, but they gave him the chance to learn what acting in front of a camera was like.

Travolta then got his first big break: the chance to play Doody, one of the characters in a touring production of *Grease*. But what of his now steady girlfriend Denise? She was too pretty to sit around waiting for her actor boyfriend to come home. She decided that the relationship – his first, and so far his only serious romance – was at an end.

YOU'RE THE ONE THAT I WANT

John enjoyed the touring production of *Grease*, although he found the work strenuous and tiring. It was fun but demanding to do the same thing night after night and still make it look fresh. So he started to look for other avenues to explore.

He had already played a few small parts on TV, so whenever he had a break from

Grease, he would fly to Los Angeles and audition for television shows there. He landed a few roles, including parts in *Rookies* and *Emergency*. They were small parts, but they all helped him to gain experience in front of the camera.

The tour of *Grease* ended. But the end brought some wonderful news for John: he was offered the chance to play Doody on Broadway. This was a big step forward for him, and he accepted at once. Some of the other actors in the touring cast were also offered roles, including a pretty young actress called Marilu Henner who by now had become very close to John. By the time they arrived in New York, John and Marilu were an item, and moved into a flat together.

Even while he was working on Broadway, John still kept a look-out for other work. He flew twice to Los Angeles to audition for a role in a movie called *The Last Detail*. The film was to star Jack Nicholson and Travolta desperately wanted the role. But though he gave the reading his all, the part went to someone else. However, the casting director who saw his audition was extremely impressed by his talents. Travolta didn't know this at the time, and deeply disappointed, he flew back to New York.

When *Grease* ended, he went straight into another Broadway show called *Over Here*, starring The Andrews Sisters. By now his salary was large enough for him to be able to indulge a long-held interest. John started taking flying lessons at New York's

Teterboro Airport, hoping to gain a private pilot's licence.

When *Over Here* finished, he was offered a role in a Broadway show called *The Ritz*. It brought with it a $600-a-week pay cheque: the largest salary the 20-year-old John had ever been offered. But Bob LeMond told him to turn it down. He advised him to head for Hollywood and start auditioning for film roles.

Travolta, still somewhat perplexed by the advice, headed for California. He did indeed win a movie role: he had two lines in a film called *The Devil's Rain*. But better things were just around the corner. He also won a role in a hospital soap called *Medical Center*, and was spotted by a producer called

James Komack. Komack was producing a new sitcom called *Welcome Back Kotter*. And a friend of his, the casting director Lynn Stalmaster, had recommended that he should see a young lad called John Travolta, who had read so well for a part in a film called *The Last Detail*. So Komack turned on the television that night and watched carefully. When he switched off, he knew he had found just what he was looking for.

Welcome Back Kotter was to be set in a school, where a group of juvenile delinquents called The Sweathogs constantly try to get the better of their teacher, Mr Kotter. The role Komack had in mind for John Travolta was as a character called Vinnie Barbarino – a none-too-bright Italian kid, who dreams one day of being in the mafia.

Travolta thought it was such a good part that he could hardly believe it when Komack told him he'd got the job.

With the part came immediate fame. *Welcome Back Kotter* proved an immediate success; on television everyone could see that The Sweathogs – the young kids who acted so tough – weren't really that macho after all. In fact, they were very funny. Overnight, Travolta found himself inundated with fan mail, from girls as young as 8 to grannies as old as 80. By the summer of 1976, Travolta was receiving over 10,000 fan letters a week.

1976 was the year that everything started happening for Travolta – personally *and* professionally. In his summer break from playing Vinnie Barbarino, Travolta appeared in a made-for-television movie called *The Boy in the Plastic Bubble*. An unashamed tear-jerker, he was cast as a teenager called Todd who – born with no natural immunity – is virtually a prisoner inside his plastic bubble tent. Casting an attractive actor in the role only added to the pathos during the scenes where Todd fell in love with a neighbouring teenage girl, but was unable to go near her.

As it happened, Travolta himself fell in love while making the film. But it wasn't with his 'screen' girlfriend. It was with the actress Diana Hyland who, 18 years older than him, was playing his mother. This was to be the start of one of the great love affairs of his life.

Diana had a vitality he found infectious. At the time he met her, she was fighting a battle against cancer, and had already had one breast removed. But she still had guts and spirit, and Travolta loved her for it. Within months of their first meeting, Diana and her three-year-old son Zachary (by a previous marriage) had moved into John's apartment in West Hollywood, and started talking about buying a house together.

That year, 1976, also brought another film – *Carrie*, the landmark horror film about a plain schoolgirl with supernatural powers. Travolta had a central part in the film, as one of Carrie's rowdy classmates who arranges to tip a bucket of pig's blood all over her at a school dance.

Meanwhile, Travolta had also been spotted by a producer called Allan Carr. Carr just happened to be watching television one day in a New York hotel room when he saw Travolta in *Welcome Back Kotter*. Carr was a show business manager who wanted to move into films. Together with his partner Robert Stigwood, he had bought the rights to make the movie of *Grease*. And as soon as he saw Travolta, Carr knew he had found his leading man. But there was a problem. Because the Broadway show of *Grease* was doing so well, Carr and Stigwood weren't allowed to make the film until after it finished its run, three years away. By that time the movie would present no competition to the stage production.

Undaunted, Carr and Stigwood signed

At the disco, *Saturday Night Fever*

Travolta anyway, and looked for another film he could act in while they waited to start work on *Grease*. They found a drama about a sulky Brooklyn stud called Tony Manero whose only escape from his dead-end job in a paint store is at the Saturday night disco. The film was to be called *Saturday Night Fever*.

Travolta was excited by the project. This was going to be his first ever leading role, and it was going to be a demanding one. Tony Manero was the dance king of the 2001 Odyssey Disco, and Travolta was going to have to look every bit as talented as Manero was meant to be. So it was back to dance lessons with a vengeance. In the run-up to filming he trained for three hours a day, using every trick that he had learnt from the black kids at school. He wasn't to know it, but the dances he performed on the screen, like the Hustle – all swivelling heels and pointing fingers – were soon to be copied in discos across the States and Europe.

When filming started, everything seemed to be going well. John had never been happier than he was with Diana. He planned to take a long holiday with her as soon as shooting was over. But then fate intervened. Suddenly, Diana - who had been in remission from her cancer – began to feel ill again. She tried to conceal how ill she felt from John, who was on location in New York and working hard. In between scenes he would phone Diana to find out how she was. She tried to sound cheerful and talk of the future, but in March 1977 he received a phone call advising him that he should return to her house in California immediately. He did so, to find her lying desperately ill.

She managed to join him for a brief walk around the garden. The following day, as they sat together, she told him she was hungry, and asked if he would buy a Japanese take-away for them to eat for dinner. He went out to do so. When he came back with the food 40 minutes later, she was lying unconscious, and later died in his arms. 'I felt the breath go out of her,' John said.

GREASE IS THE WORD

After Diana's death, John had very little time to mourn. He attended her funeral, dressed in a white suit he had bought especially for the holiday they had planned to take in Rio. Then he had to fly straight back to New York, to continue shooting *Saturday Night Fever*.

The journey back from Los Angeles to New York was torture for him. 'I would do anything in the world for her death not to have happened,' he told friends. With Diana gone, the centre of his world had been wiped out. And not even Scientology, the controversial religion he had been introduced to by actress Joan Prather on the set of *The Devil's Rain*, could cure his deepest hurt. Desperately upset, he managed to get a first-class seat on the flight, so at least he had some privacy from the prying eyes of fans. But once the plane was airborne, he broke down and sobbed.

He later realised he was being watched; not by just anyone, but by the cult artist and film-maker Andy Warhol, who was the only other passenger in the first-class cabin. He peered curiously through the seats at Travolta as he wept. 'I thought, I don't want to be watched when this is happening,' John revealed later. 'It was a strange scene.'

When he reached New York, however, the cast and crew of the film rallied round him. They let him know that they had clubbed together and sent a donation to a cancer research charity in memory of Diana: a thoughtful gesture that touched him greatly. Even his chauffeur came to his aid, working six days a week instead of five, because he didn't trust his Saturday stand-in to look after John properly.

With their support, John was able to get on with filming the movie that was to be his breakthrough. Ironically, *Saturday Night Fever* was never intended to be a hit; producers Stigwood and Carr had only meant it to pass the time until they could make the movie they really wanted – *Grease*. Even in the run up to the release of *Saturday Night Fever*, they didn't realise what excitement they were about to unleash.

The story of Tony Manero was based on a newspaper article about the young men of Brooklyn who worked at dead-end jobs during the day, had problems at home, and could only really let off steam on Saturdays at the disco. Tony Manero was an amalgam of these disaffected youngsters.

The film reflected the boredom and disaffection that many people felt, and when it was released it proved to be one of those rare movies that finds a place in the popular consciousness at the right time. Within days of

Grease: Travolta and Olivia Newton-John

its opening, discos suddenly found themselves at the forefront of a new craze. Audiences left the cinema aching to go and strut their stuff; suddenly dance teachers who had been struggling for pupils found themselves inundated with inquiries from new students.

The film's biggest impact was on men: the dance floor had always been the territory of the disco queen, but now it was considered all right to be a disco king as well. Discos were flooded by a crowd of John Travolta wannabes, who swapped their week-day suits and greasy overalls for flared trousers, tightly fitted jackets, and smartly slicked-back hair. They all wanted to look like John Travolta and dance The Hustle as well as he did.

Suddenly Travolta was a mega-star. Crowds queued for hours at the cinema to see the film, and thousands tried to gate-crash the premiere party in New York.

Travolta's career was made: and more importantly, so was his fortune. He had always been smart with cash, investing his savings from the very earliest days when he had been making a few thousand dollars a time in commercials. He now pulled off a canny financial deal: although his salary for the film was just $150,000 – a fraction of the $350 million *Saturday Night Fever* would eventually make – he asked for a cut of the profits from sales of the soundtrack album. He was either incredibly clever or incredibly lucky, as this move made him a millionaire ten times over. He says he was just careful: 'I've

Greased Lightning!

watched people I know take big risks and some lost at it. I'm willing to do that with my career, but not with my money,' he said.

The film didn't just make him a star: it also made Hollywood take him seriously as an actor. At first, the film establishment were inclined to scoff at a movie in which a sitcom star bopped around a disco. They subsequently ate their words. In December 1977, Travolta was named Best Actor by the National Board of Review, and nominated in the same category for a Golden Globe award. Then in February 1978, just before the film opened in Britain, he heard the news that he had been nominated for the Best Actor award at that year's Oscars. Aged 24, high school drop-out, John was suddenly considered good enough to compete for Hollywood's top accolade with Richard Burton, Richard Dreyfuss, Woody Allen and Marcello Mastroianni.

He didn't win: the coveted statuette went that year to Richard Dreyfuss (for *The Goodbye Girl*). But John decided that just to be nominated for this prestigious prize was good enough for him. It meant he had joined a pretty exclusive club.

By the time of the Oscars ceremony, John already had his next film, *Grease*, under his belt. Despite many people's scepticism, audiences turned up in even greater numbers than they had to see *Saturday Night Fever*. They loved the romance between the king of cool, Danny Zuko (Travolta) and the clean-living, fresh-faced Sandy (Olivia

Stepping out with Olivia, *Grease*

Newton-John). She was spotted by Allan Carr when he went to a party one night, and saw a pretty girl across the room from him pulling cheeky faces at a friend. It helped, of course, that the leading role was taken by Hollywood's newest star.

The film was a hit, with Olivia Newton-John's 'Summer Nights' topping the charts for weeks, and it sealed John's status as a new icon. *Grease* was even more successful in financial terms than *Saturday Night Fever*, earning $400 million.

Suddenly John's face was everywhere. It was on the cover of *Time* magazine, which unbent from its usual study of world political events to dissect 'Travolta Fever'. It also appeared on dolls and games which sold like hot cakes. He even found himself invited to the White House to dine with President Carter. 'Travolta Fever' spread throughout Europe as well: in London, at the British premiere of Grease, fans charged his car in Leicester Square; in Paris, thousands picketed his hotel room.

On screen, leather-jacketed Danny and clean-cut Sandy loved and lost, and loved again. 'You're The One That I Want', they sang to each other. Off screen, it was a similar story. Travolta, single again after Diana's death, fell for Olivia, and fell heavily. But she was very wary about being seen in public with him: after all, she had to convince the public that she was a nice, moral, virginal sort of girl. She consented to dating Travolta in private for four months.

He was so smitten that he even proposed marriage to her, but she turned him down. Once again, he was heart-broken.

However, even if his love life was disastrous, at least his bank balance was healthy. After the success of *Saturday Night Fever*, his salary for making *Grease* had shot up from $150,000 to $500,000. More importantly, his deal giving him a cut from the sales of the soundtrack albums was still in place. Between them, sales of the albums of both *Grease* and *Saturday Night Fever* now topped 19 million copies, making Travolta very wealthy indeed. Ultimately, the profits from soundtrack sales would top a billion dollars – although the money didn't all go to Travolta. It went to his accountants and his lawyers as well.

In his personal life, Travolta now faced more tragedy. Following the death of his lover Diana Hyland from cancer, within a year his mother Helen was dead too, and by cruel coincidence, she was a victim of the same disease.

The two deaths, coming so close together, really knocked him for six. 'John had just become one of the most famous people in the world, and extraordinarily wealthy,' his sister Ellen told a friend. 'But the people he was closest to in his personal life were gone.' Travolta went home to New Jersey to see his brothers and sisters, and together they comforted each other and tried to work out their grief over their mother's death.

But it was too much for John. The combination of extraordinary professional success and terrible personal loss led them to behave in ways that seemed out of character. He tried to assuage his grief with a massive spending spree: he bought himself three private planes, a fleet of expensive cars and splashed out over a million pounds on a home in Santa Barbara, California. And then he began to act like a Hollywood mogul. 'He was still a baby to us,' says Ellen. 'But he would sit at the head of a long, long table, summoning his servants with a buzzer he worked with his foot. This was definitely *not* the way he had been brought up.'

Saturday Night Fever had made John a star almost overnight, and *Grease* had cemented his fame. But after his mother's death, he

Urban Cowboy

entered a phase when almost everything he did went wrong. After playing several punk characters – Vinnie Barbarino, Tony Manero, Danny Zuko were all from the 'wrong' side of town – Travolta decided on a change of image. He felt it was time to do a different kind of film, like a love story with the respected Hollywood star Lily Tomlin, one of his favourite actresses. But the chemistry between the two of them didn't convince audiences. *Moment by Moment*, as it was called, bombed.

His next film, *Urban Cowboy*, in which that sweet smile and wavy hair were topped off by a big Texan hat, redeemed Travolta's reputation for a while, but after that he plunged into a string of best forgotten films. The problem wasn't so much that he was offered bad films, but that he failed to recognise good parts when they were offered to him. In 1979, the year after *Grease*, he was offered the leading role in *American Gigolo*, an intriguing thriller about a male escort who is framed for a murder he didn't commit. He turned it down.

In 1981, Travolta was offered another leading role: that of a poor kid who goes through hell training for the American forces in *An Officer and a Gentleman*. Both parts, after he refused them, went to Richard Gere, who became a star on the back of them. Subsequently, John turned down starring parts in *Midnight Express* and in the mermaid comedy *Splash* – which made a big splash for the man who did accept the role, Tom Hanks. So what was

John Travolta up to? Was he trying to end his own career?

STAYING ALIVE

John went on working throughout the eighties. But his luck had changed. Nothing he touched turned to gold: the films became turkeys instead.

The problem was that John didn't really know what kind of movies he wanted to make. He put on a brave and cheerful face, although inside he was afraid and confused, even having ulcers because of the pressure to make films that didn't exploit his image. But he wouldn't admit it.

And so he ploughed on from one forgettable film to another. Some had promise but just didn't work out, such as *Blow Out*, a thriller by Brian de Palma (who had directed *Carrie*) about a sound recordist who thinks he may have taped an assassination. Travolta thought he had done good work in the film, but it failed to find an audience.

So he made some more obvious crowd pleasers – like the *Saturday Night Fever* sequel *Staying Alive*, and the *Grease* follow-up *Two of Kind*, in which Travolta teamed up again with Olivia Newton-John to play two musical bankrobbers. Both somehow failed to ignite the spark created by the original films.

Blow Out

After this the flops continued. John never lost faith in his own talent but the films went on bombing. He took part in duds like *Perfect*, a film which was little more than an excuse to show the exquisite body of Jamie Lee Curtis working out in the gym. One bright spot of the eighties was being invited to the White House in 1985 to a dinner attended by the Prince and Princess of Wales. Travolta got to whirl Princess Diana round the floor, and was thrilled. He told friends afterwards he had found her so stunning that he hadn't been able to say a word to her.

It wasn't until 1989 that his life gradually started to come together again. *The Experts* – another forgettable movie about a town full of Russian spies – didn't set the box office

With Olivia Newton-John again in *Two of a Kind*

alight, but it did re-awaken Travolta's private life. He'd become so depressed about his career that he had gone back to flying school, and had obtained a licence to fly jets. He was seriously considering throwing in the towel and becoming a pilot instead, when he met Kelly Preston, his young and pretty co-star. He first saw her at the auditions, where something about her reminded him slightly of Diana Hyland. But he didn't make a move on her straightaway. After all, she was married at the time.

However, when they flew to Canada and started working on the film, John discovered her marriage was in trouble. He began to talk to her about Scientology, the controversial religion he had discovered some years earlier. He felt that it had helped him carry on when he was in anguish over career problems and upsets in his personal life; he started passing on some of his beliefs to Kelly, hoping Scientology would help her, too. As filming continued, they grew closer, and gradually they fell in love.

Kelly was intrigued by Travolta. For one thing, this famous man was in his late thirties and still unmarried – something that made her wonder if there was anything in the rumours (which occasionally arose about him) that he was gay. But when they eventually went to bed with each other, it scotched her doubts on that score. 'He is one of the world's greatest lovers,' she said, 'and he made me feel I was the only woman on earth for him. I fell in love with him in days.' John in turn was ecstatic about his

John with Kelly Preston, his future wife, in *The Experts*

new found happiness. He had been lonely for too long, and too many relationships – such as with Marilu Henner and Olivia Newton-John – had not worked out.

Meanwhile, his acting career was looking up as well. He signed up to make *Look Who's Talking*, a weird-sounding comedy about a talking baby. John played the friendly taxi driver who arrives in single mother Kirstie Alley's life, when he drives her to hospital to give birth and then stays around and becomes an adoptive dad. Despite its bizarre premise it became a hit, pulling in enough punters to convince the studios to make not one but two sequels.

Travolta enjoyed the first in the series, and the second one in which a talking baby girl

The taxi driver, *Look Who's Talking*

arrives (*Look Who's Talking Too*). By the third film, *Look Who's Talking Now*, in which dogs did the talking, he was less happy. But at least the money was rolling in again.

He bought a house with Kelly on the coast in Penobscot, in America's eastern state of Maine. He also bought a holiday home in Daytona Beach, Florida and an 80-foot Gulfstream Jet, figuring that little Lear jets were too small for him now he was no longer a bachelor, but part of a happy couple. He liked to describe his Gulfstream as his own personal 'house in the clouds'.

The eighties became the 1990s, and although the *Look Who's Talking* films weren't great movies, John didn't care too much. He

Travolta and Kirstie Alley in *Look Who's Talking Now*

was too happy in his home life, especially in 1991 when Kelly told him she was pregnant. Ecstatic, he whisked her off to Paris in September, where they married in a quiet midnight ceremony.

In 1992, Kelly gave birth to a son. John was overjoyed. They named him Jett, because of John's fascination with planes, and built an incredible Wonderland Wing for him in their Florida holiday home, with an ice-cream parlour, a mini-theatre, and a bedroom built in the shell of a real plane.

Towards the end of 1992, Travolta was involved in a terrifying incident when a technical fault blacked out all the instruments and the radio on the plane. Flying blind through the clouds, the plane narrowly missed a Boeing 727 with 180 passengers on board. Eventually, Travolta and a co-pilot managed to land the Gulfstream safely, but he was badly shaken: worried not so much about himself as about Kelly and seven-month-old Jett who were both asleep on board at the time.

The near miss seemed an apt metaphor for John's career, which was foundering once again. Apart from the makers of the third *Look Who's Talking* film, nobody was knocking at Travolta's door. Until, out of the blue, he got a phone call from *wunderkind* film director, Quentin Tarantino.

Tarantino was the hot young director of *Reservoir Dogs*, a bloody movie about a jewel robbery gone wrong. It had won

John as Vincent Vega in *Pulp Fiction*

huge critical acclaim and its overnight success had propelled the young moviemaker into the mainstream. He rang Travolta to ask if they could have lunch together.

At lunch, Travolta discovered that Quentin had long been a fan of his. He bombarded Travolta with questions about his career, and particularly about his favourite director Brian De Palma – with whom Travolta had made *Carrie* and *Blow Out*. A few weeks later, when *Reservoir Dogs* star Michael Madsen suddenly had to drop out of Quentin's new movie *Pulp Fiction*, Tarantino was on the phone, offering John Travolta a role as a junkie hit man. To Tarantino, it seemed an inspired bit of casting to have the eternally nice John Travolta play a bad man. But in order to land him the role of Vincent Vega, he had to fight hard.

For one thing, the production company backing *Pulp Fiction*, Miramax, thought Tarantino was gambling his entire movie by involving John. Every time Tarantino mentioned John Travolta's name, studio executives would say, 'You cast *who*?'

For another, he had to convince Travolta to play the part. John had worries about the moral message of *Pulp Fiction*, a violent film in which Vincent Vega is seen taking heroin and 'accidentally' blowing a man's head off in the back of the car. Eventually both Travolta and Miramax said yes, with Travolta accepting a salary of a mere $150,000 – the same amount he had

Samuel L. Jackson and Travolta in *Pulp Fiction*

received 20 years before for *Saturday Night Fever*. It turned out to be one of the best decisions he ever made.

Pulp Fiction thrilled Tarantino's fans. A complex, blackly funny, three-part story of gangsters and their girls, drug addicts, bent boxers, and a mystery suitcase containing something the audience is never allowed to see, it went down a storm. Its mix of horror and humour had audiences on the edge of their seats, and it became *the* most talked about film of 1994. Travolta himself was a revelation, putting all his natural charm into a performance as an affable, doped-up murderer that made the critics sit up and take notice of him for the first time in over a decade.

Suddenly, Travolta was hot property again. Audiences loved seeing him in such a different role: they whooped at the scene in which, high on heroin, he gets up on a restaurant dance floor and starts doing The Twist – an ironic reference to *Saturday Night Fever* which nobody missed. When the film scooped the top prize at the 1994 Cannes Film Festival, it was just the start of a long string of awards that it would win. The award culminated in a Best Actor Oscar nomination in February 1995.

In the event, Travolta didn't win it: Tom Hanks was the lucky recipient. But it hardly mattered. For by now, Travolta's career was experiencing another astonishing, meteoric rise. He was quickly signed up to make *Get Shorty*, an adaptation of an Elmore Leonard novel about a loan shark who goes to collect the cash from a client one day, and ends up being talked into becoming a movie producer. Danny De Vito was to produce the film, but at first, Travolta refused the role. He had just played a gangster and he didn't want to play another one. But then his friend Quentin Tarantino rang him and urged him to accept. So he did: for a salary that had now risen sharply to $5 million. The movie again set tongues wagging in Hollywood, and in January 1996 he was rewarded with a Golden Globe award for his performance. The only thing that grieved Travolta this time was having to shed a stone for the role. 'It was damn hard. I like my food,' he revealed afterwards.

It now looks as though the sky is once again

John Travolta in *Get Shorty*

the limit for Travolta. He turned in a beautifully stylish performance as the super-cool villain of an action film called *Broken Arrow*. Then in early 1996, it was announced that he had become the highest paid film star in history, after signing a deal that would net twenty million and one dollars to make a film aptly called *The Phenomenon*. (The extra one dollar just pushes him past Sylvester Stallone in the list of 'highest paid leading men'.)

The man, who three years ago was wondering when his phone would ring, is suddenly being inundated with offers. And he is delighted. Looking back on the ups and downs of his life, Travolta muses: 'It's fair to say, there was a time when I thought to myself "It's all over". Now, some days, I have to pinch myself to make sure it's real.'

FILMOGRAPHY

The year refers to the first release date of the film

1975 The Devil's Rain
1976 The Boy in the Plastic Bubble
1976 Carrie
1977 Saturday Night Fever
1978 Grease
1979 Moment by Moment
1980 Urban Cowboy

Staying Alive

1981	Blow Out
1983	Staying Alive
1983	Two of a Kind
1985	Perfect
1987	The Dumb Waiter
1989	The Experts
1989	Look Who's Talking
1990	Chains of Gold
1990	Look Who's Talking Too
1991	Midnight Rider
1991	Shout
1993	Look Who's Talking Now
1994	Pulp Fiction
1995	Get Shorty
1995	White Man's Burden
1996	Broken Arrow
1996	Michael
1996	The Double

ACKNOWLEDGEMENTS

Aquarius
Columbia (courtesy Kobal)
Miramax (courtesy Kobal)
Paramount (courtesy Kobal)
Tri-Star (courtesy Kobal)
20th Century Fox (courtesy Kobal)